GUITAR ATLAS SERIES

Guitar Styles from Around the Globe

Flamenco

Your passport to a new world of music

DENNIS KOSTER

Alfred, the leader in educational publishing,

and the National Guitar Workshop,

one of America's finest guitar schools, have joined

forces to bring you the best, most progressive

educational tools possible. We hope you will enjoy

this book and encourage you to look for

other fine products from Alfred and the

National Guitar Workshop.

Copyright © MMII by Alfred Publishing Co., Inc.
All rights reserved. Printed in USA.

ISBN 0-7390-2478-7 (Book and CD)

This book was acquired, edited and produced
by Workshop Arts, Inc., the publishing arm of
the National Guitar Workshop.
Nathaniel Gunod, acquisitions and editor
Michael Rodman, editor
Matt Cramer, music typesetting
Timothy Phelps, interior design
CD recorded at Gizmo Enterprises, Inc., New York, NY
and mastered at Bar None Studios, Northford, CT
Cover photo: © Look / EStock Photo, LLC
Interior illustrations: Dennis Koster

Contents

0 **Track 1** A compact disc is included with this book. This disc can make learning with the book easier and more enjoyable. The symbol shown at the left appears next to every example that is on the CD. Use the CD to help ensure that you're capturing the feel of the examples, interpreting the rhythms correctly, and so on. The track number below the symbol corresponds directly to the example you want to hear. Track 1 will help you tune your guitar to this CD.

About the Author

Dennis Koster's New York debut was hailed in the New York Times as "a considerable success … a brilliant, aptly fantastic performance." One of New York's most sought after teachers for over 25 years, Dennis has guest lectured and performed at the Peabody Conservatory, the Juilliard School, the American String Teachers Association, and the New York Bach Gesellscaft. A brilliant classical guitarist and flamenco player in equal measure, Mr. Koster studied with Juan D. Grecos, Mario Escudero and the legendary Sabicas, who called him "an excellent interpreter of my compositions." He has toured extensively in the U.S. and Japan, and has been broadcast throughout Spain. A frequent artist at the National Guitar Workshop, Dennis teaches in New York City and is the author of the three-volume method, *The Keys to Falmenco Guitar*. His classical and flamenco CDs are on the Music Masters label of the Musical Heritage Society.

Pronunciation Guide

Aire	= EYE-ray
Alegrias	= ah-leh-GREE-ahs
Alzapua	= ahl-thah-POO-ah
Apoyando	= a-poh-YAHN-doh
Baile	= BUY-ee
Bulerias	= boo-leh-REE-ahs
Cante	= KAHN-tay
Escobillas	= es-coh-BEE-yahs
Falseta	= fahl-SET-ah
Fandangos	= fahn-DAHN-gohs
Farrucus	= fah-ROO-kah
Golpe	= GOL-pay
Golpeador	= gohl-pee-AH-dohr
Granadinas	= grahn-ah-DEEN-ahs
Huelva	= WELL-vah
Jondo	= HON-doh
Llamada	= ya-MAH-dah
Madre	= MAH-dray
Picado	= pee-CAH-doh
Rasgueado	= rahs-gay-AH-doh
Remata	= ray-MAH-tah
Siguiriyas	= sih-geh-REE-ahs
Soleares	= sol-aye-ARE-es
Soledad	= sol-aye-dahd
Tangos	= tahn-GOHS
Tarantas	= tah-RAHN-tas
Toque	= TOKE
Verdiales	= vair-dee-AH-less

Introduction

In the minds of many guitarists, flamenco is "the king of guitar styles," combining the most appealing aspects of all guitar playing: Its spectacular, driving rhythms rival the most exciting popular styles; it shares improvisational freedom and great harmonic sophistication with jazz; it equals the musical depth and complete right-hand technique of classical guitar; and today's flamenco players perform with a level of virtuosity that leaves even heavy metal players breathless.

What was once an art limited to the narrow confines of ethnic boundaries—the Gypsies of southern Spain—today, flamenco is played all over the world by guitarists whose enthusiasm appears limitless. Many are first drawn to flamenco by exposure to superficial "pop-flamenco" styles; many begin playing flamenco by "faking it" in an attempt to "sound Spanish." But, oh-so-often, these same guitarists, once they've heard the real thing, forget all that is fake and devote themselves to learning authentic flamenco.

From classical to rock, guitarists of other styles often express frustration about solving the mysteries of flamenco: "How can that technique *possibly* be done?" or, "I could *never* learn that complex rhythm," and so on. It's my goal to answer all of your questions about flamenco and have you experience the thrill of playing true flamenco guitar.

This introduction to flamenco is designed for guitarists who have some classical training or are adept at fingerstyle playing. This book also assumes that you read standard music notation and/or tablature and that you have a good understanding of the fundamentals of harmony and rhythm.

In this book, we'll explore the complex strumming techniques of flamenco as well as flamenco percussion effects, thumb technique, arpeggios, tremolos, *picado* (flamenco scales), and performance style.

Not only is flamenco guitar technique complex, the art of flamenco itself is complex, encompassing literally dozens of songs and dances from nearly every region of Spain. In this book you will sample many different flamenco forms, but in an effort to provide some depth into the study, the lion's share of the forms will be from the "first family of flamenco rhythms"—the *soleares* family, which includes *soleares, alegrías,* and *bulerías*. All the techniques explained will be applied to these three rhythms, building your flamenco vocabulary and leading to three concert-level solos at the conclusion of the book. These solos incorporate all the techniques, rhythms, and melodic variations explained in these pages. Along the way, many other flamenco forms will be introduced in short examples.

The Guitar Atlas series welcomes you to Spain and the thrilling world of flamenco guitar.

The Guitar in Flamenco

Flamenco is the art of the Andalusian Gypsies—their song (*cante*), dance (*baile*), and guitar playing (*toque*). Although its origins go back hundreds of years to the time of Ferdinand and Isabelle, flamenco as we know it emerged in southern Spain during the mid-19th century.

In its early history, the guitar in flamenco was a humble accompaniment to the song and dance, which were considered far greater arts, if the guitar was considered an art at all! By the turn of the century, guitarists such as Maestro Patiño began to give a more expressive voice to the guitar, but it was not until the 1930s that flamenco guitar achieved recognition as the expressive equal of the song and dance. Ramón Montoya revolutionized flamenco guitar. A friend of classical master Miguel Llobet, Montoya not only brought classical guitar technique to flamenco—all the arpeggios, scales, tremolos, and so on—but the *language* of classical music as well. Montoya was the first to perform solo flamenco guitar concerts. His Paris concerts during the Spanish Civil War caused a sensation. His style was further developed by followers Niño Ricardo and concert artists Sabicas and Mario Escudero, who performed solo flamenco guitar in the great concert halls of the world.

In the 1970s, another revolution took place in flamenco. Paco de Lucía, who, in his early 20s, was already considered one of history's greatest guitarists, created a new modern style of flamenco incorporating the harmonic language of progressive jazz and a sophisticated Latin-influenced approach to traditional rhythms. Paco's revolution inspired an entire new generation of flamenco artists in Spain, where there are now more high-caliber flamenco artists than at any other time in history, largely due to the enormous influence of Paco de Lucía.

Flamenco can be played on any nylon-string guitar as long as it is equipped with some type of a *golpeador* (tap-plate or top-guard, similar to the pickguard on a steel-string acoustic guitar), to protect the guitar from stylistic rhythmic tapping. Traditional flamenco guitars are cypress bodied, have low action and a more percussive and brilliant sound than classical guitars.

Flamenco players are very casual about their sitting positions. Most sit cross legged, many use footstools, and some sit in the traditional Gypsy position with both feet on the floor and the lower bout of the guitar resting on the right thigh.

Flamenco left-hand technique is identical to that of classical guitar; right-hand position is only modified as needed to perform specific flamenco techniques. Fingernails are used to play flamenco just as they are in classical guitar.

The very best way to learn flamenco is to accompany flamenco dancers, and later, flamenco singers. If there are no flamenco artists near you, listen to all the flamenco recordings you possibly can—not just modern flamenco, but also historical recordings of the past masters and especially the cante.

Traditional Gypsy position

Chapter 1   FLAMENCO FORMS AND RASGUEADO

SPAIN

RASGUEADO

Flamenco strumming technique is called *rasgueado*. A remarkable variety of rasgueado techniques are applied to flamenco rhythms—and the resulting sound can be electrifying. To most guitarists, expertly played rasgueado sounds like almost impossible virtuosity, but the technique can be broken down into basic movements, which can be learned through patient practice.

Rasgueado strokes are played by extensor muscles (the muscles that extend the fingers). Outside of flamenco, these muscles are rarely used in guitar playing. Their strength and agility must be developed carefully over time. It takes about one year of intelligent practice to master basic rasgueado techniques.

One of the biggest mistakes a flamenco student can make is to equate excessive force with the fire they hear in great rasgueado playing. Flamenco masters play rasgueado effortlessly. The fire comes from their expression.

Never strain or use excessive force when playing rasgueado technique. Great rasgueado is played by relaxed hands using free unrestrained motions learned through patient practice—*not* by brute force!

Right-Hand Fingers
Thumb .... *p*
Index .... *i*
Middle .... *m*
Ring .... *a*
Little (pinky) .. *e*

LESSON 1—RASGUEADO WITH *i*

In flamenco playing, the rhythm is often marked by downstrokes and upstrokes of the index finger (*i*), which uses a free, swinging motion from the large knuckle joint (the joint that connects the finger to the hand). This technique is performed from a steady and comfortable hand position in which the thumb (*p*) rests on the 6th string to balance and support the hand. When *i* alone plays rasgueado strokes, the little (*e*), ring (*a*), and middle (*m*) fingers remain passively extended and are never curled into the palm.

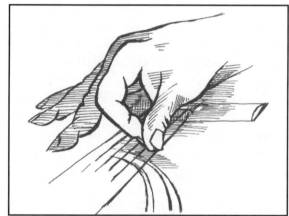

Starting position: *i* is folded in toward the palm; *e*, *a*, and *m* are extended passively.

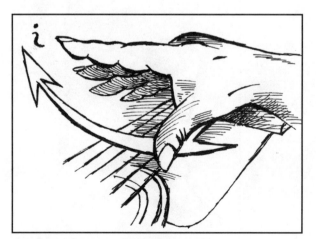

1. Downstroke: *i* extends fully with a free, swinging motion.

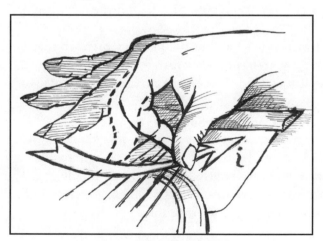

2. Upstroke: *i* returns to its starting position, brushing (not hooking) the strings.

COMPÁS

Compás, which means "rhythm," may be the most important word used in flamenco. Its meaning subtly changes depending on the context in which it is used. Compás can describe rhythm in general, or it can be used to describe the specific rhythmic structure of a flamenco form. For example, in this lesson, we will be learning the compás of soleares. Compás can also be used to describe the individual phrase of a flamenco form. Example 2 on page 8, for instance, is one compás of soleares, whereas example 3 includes two compáses.

SOLEARES

The Gypsies call *soleares* "*La Madre de Cante*" ("The Mother of Song"), as it is generally considered the oldest form of flamenco. Soleares derives its name from the Spanish word *soledad*, which means either "loneliness" or "solitude." A slow and serious song, soleares is an example of flamenco's *cante jondo* or deep song. Its lyrics are among the most moving and profound in Spanish poetry.

In the exotic key of E Phrygian (the scale you hear when playing all natural notes from E to E), typical chords in soleares are shown below. Notice that the E chord in the last bar is major. This is typical, even though the other chords are clearly Phrygian (a minor mode).

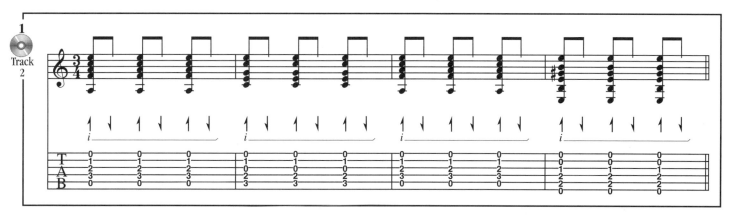

NOTE:
In flamenco music notation, it is customary to show all of the notes in a rasgueado chord only once per beam. Further occurances of the chord under that beam are indicated with a noteless stem.

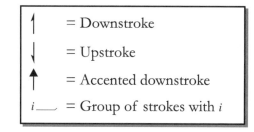

THE COMPÁS OF SOLEARES

Soleares and the dances that derive from it, *alegrías* and *bulerías*, share a very distinctive rhythmic structure. Often written in 3/4 time for easier reading, soleares is actually performed in 12-beat phrases with a very specific series of accents:

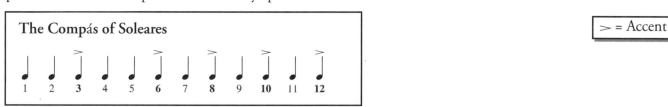

> = Accent

See Lesson 5 on page 14 for a more in-depth study of this rhythmic structure.

Adding accents on beats 3, 6, 8, 10, and 12 transforms an exercise of steady eighth notes into true flamenco. Play accented downstrokes with slightly more force than the unaccented beats.

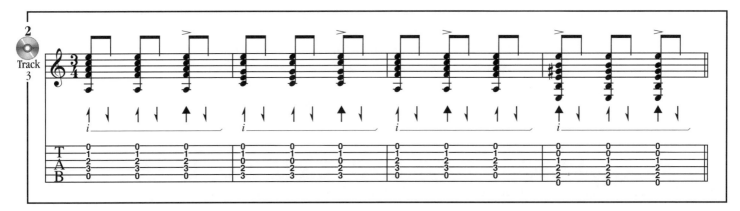

ALEGRÍAS

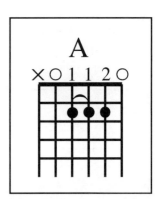

Next we turn to one of flamenco's most joyous expressions—*alegrías*, which is Spanish for "happiness." The emotional opposite of soleares, alegrías shares the same rhythmic structure but is played at a quicker tempo and in a major key. The alegrías in example 3 is in A Major. Note that flamenco guitarists use two fingers to play the first-position A Major chord; the tip section of the 1st finger covers the notes on both the 3rd and 4th strings (see the diagram on the right).

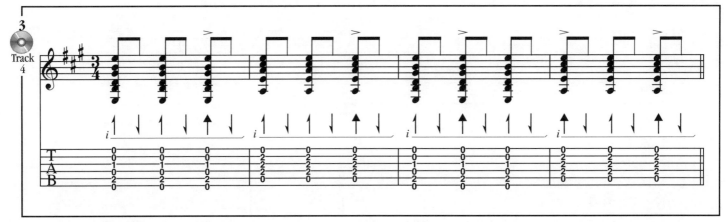

LESSON 2—FIVE-STROKE RASGUEADO

When rasgueado technique incorporates all the fingers of the right hand, it blossoms into a full language of remarkable guitar sounds and seemingly limitless rhythmic articulations. The most commonly used rasgueado, known as the Ramon Montoya rasgueado, is the five-stroke rasgueado. Four downstrokes are followed by an *i* upstroke. This rasgueado pattern is excellent for preparing the hand for other flamenco techniques.

Your ultimate goal in learning the five-stroke rasgueado is to acheive complete independence of the fingers, resulting in evenly spaced rasgueado strokes, each heard individually. The hand is held in a steady and comfortable position, the thumb resting on the 6th string for balance and support. In the starting position, the fingers are folded in toward the palm in a loose fist. The fingers are held close to the strings with the fingertips just behind the 6th string (even though the thumb is resting there). Each finger, beginning with the *e*, then *a*, *m*, and *i*, is fully extended in a series of completely independent downstrokes. Each finger completes its stroke *before* the next finger moves. The five-stroke pattern is completed by an upstroke with *i*, which brushes (rather than hooks) the strings.

> **The Five-Stroke Rasgueado Pattern**
> *e*   down
> *a*   down
> *m*   down
> *i*   down
> *i*   up

Starting position

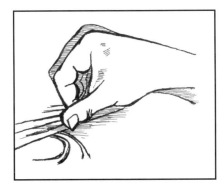

1. Downstroke with *e*

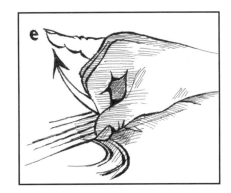

2. Downstroke with *a*

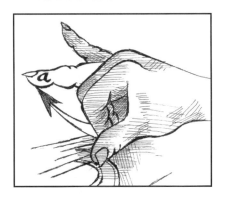

3. Downstroke with *m*

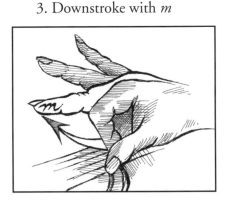

4. Downstroke with *i*

5. Upstroke with *i*

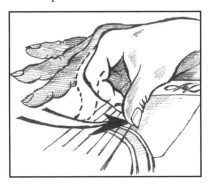

Remember that in beginning to learn five-stroke rasgueados, you will be training new muscles. Be sure to keep your hand supple and relaxed during your initial attempts at this technique. Never force or strain (it can't be mentioned often enough). As you practice five-stroke rasgueados, your finger independence and extension will develop—but this only takes place over time.

Next, we will introduce five-stroke rasgueados into the compáses of soleares and alegrías. Here, the five-stroke pattern will be used to articulate even, quintuplet rhythms (one beat divided into five equal parts). This technique will be indicated in the notation as follows:

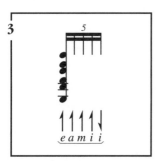

In example 4, a five-stroke rasgueado precedes each accented beat. Notice how the accents now stand out in stark contrast to the more fluid rasgueados.

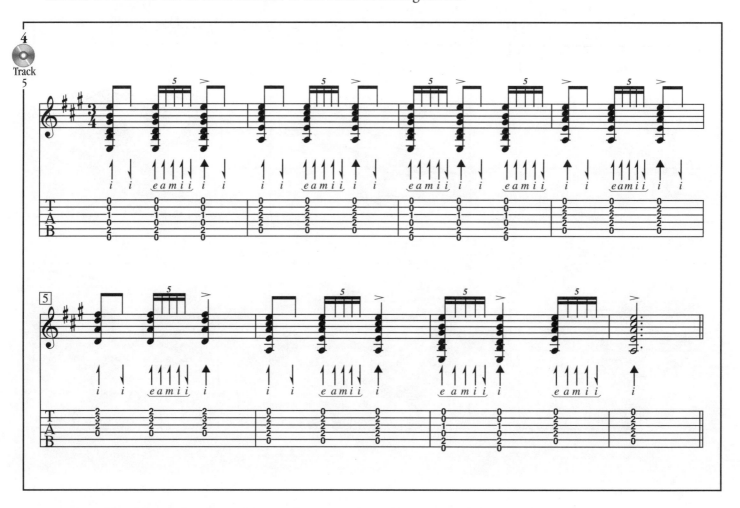

Flamenco dancers often lead into each accent with a volley of machine-gun-like *taconeo* (heelwork). The effect is very dramatic, like a giant wave cresting and then breaking. Guitarists create a similar effect by leading into accents with multiple rasgueados. The desired effect is achieved when there are no perceptible pauses between the rasgueados or the accented beats.

Here, continuous rasgueados lead into every accented beat of the soleares compás. When mastered, this rasgueado pattern reveals the true *aire* (spirit) of soleares. Note that the second compás of this example has the added spice of chord alterations, which are typical of the style.

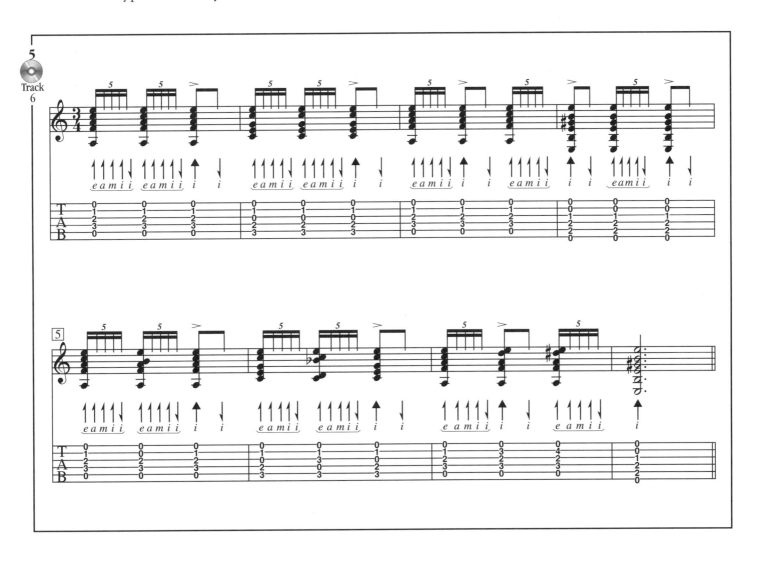

LESSON 3—THE GOLPE AND *a-m* STROKE

This lesson explores two particularly strong rhythmic expressions of flamenco guitar: the *golpe*, a percussive tap on the face of the guitar, and the *a-m* stroke in which two fingers are used as one.

GOLPE

The golpe is used to mark time during silences or to mark accents. It is used alone or adds greater emphasis to accented notes and chords. Golpes are played with the *a* finger in a motion that is almost identical to a *rest stroke* (the technique in which the striking finger lands on the adjacent lower string), except that the fingernail (not the pad of the finger) contacts the face of the guitar about one-half inch from the 1st string. Golpes are played with very little force. The face of the guitar is very responsive and produces a clear golpe sound with the lightest touch. Overly loud golpes can sound very ugly—or worse, break your fingernail!

> ♩ = Golpe alone in standard music notation
>
> ✕ = Golpe in tablature or in standard notation when combined with other notes or chords

> **Important Note:** Never play golpes on a guitar that does not have a golpeador (tap-plate or top-guard). Golpes will leave permanent scars on the face of an unprotected guitar.

Here is a very simple use of golpes combined with four-note chords to achieve a striking (pardon the pun) rhythmic effect.

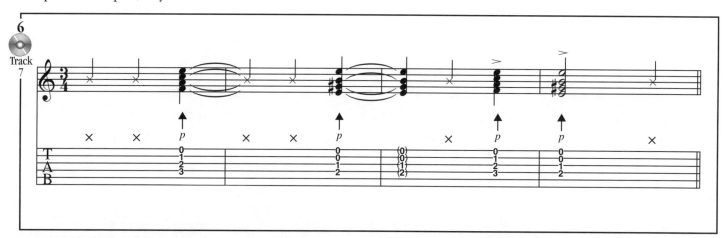

It is important to note that golpes, like much else in flamenco, are often added on the spur of the moment. It is unlikely that a flamenco guitarist would play the same piece twice and apply this technique exactly the same way both times.

THE *a-m* STROKE

The *a-m*, stroke is the loudest rasgueado stroke, using two fingers as if they were one, large finger. This stroke can be performed in two distinct manners.

1) With the hand held steady and the thumb resting on the 6th string, *m* and *a* are folded into the hand while *e* and *i* remain passively extended. Then, *m* and *a* are fully extended, striking the accented chord. This stroke is used for five-note chords.

2) An even stronger accent can be achieved by adding forearm rotation to the stroke. The entire hand moves, and the thumb does *not* rest on the 6th string. As *m* and *a* are folded into the hand, the wrist rotates so that you see into your palm. Then, as *m* and *a* are extended, the hand and arm turn so that by the time the stroke is completed, you see the back of your hand. This is a very loose, whip-like motion in which the hand is almost completely passive. *The looser the hand, the stronger the stroke.* Any rigidity in the hand or arm will weaken the sound.

The use of *a-m* strokes is essential to the accompaniment of the most important of all flamenco dance steps—the *llamada*.

LESSON 4—LLAMADA

In flamenco, it is the dancer who controls the length, speed, structure, and intensity of the dance. In almost every other form of dance, people dance to the music, but in flamenco it is the job of the guitarist—even if you're Paco de Lucía himself—to follow the dancer. An important aspect of the relationship between the flamenco dancer and guitarist is the dance step known as *llamada* (the call). In soleares, alegrías, and bulerías, large sections of the dance are brought to a close by the llamada, often marked with a strong, stamped 1–2–3, and always ending on the 10th beat of the final compás.

Just as the llamada is a specific step, there is specific music used to accompany it. Following are examples of llamadas por soleares* and alegrías. Both use strong *a-m,* strokes to match the strength of the dancer's heelwork. The golpe on the 4th beat of each example is very typical in llamada accompaniment.

Llamada por Soleares

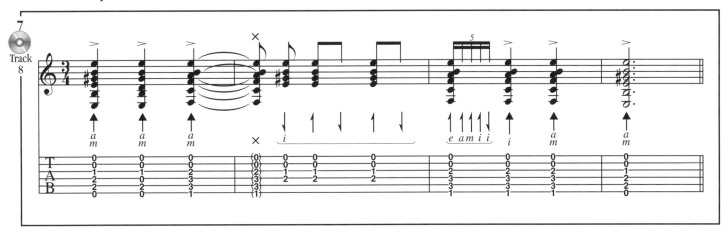

Llamada por Alegrías

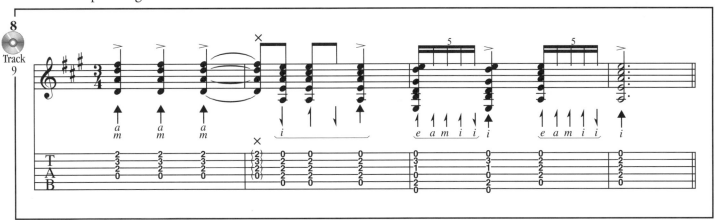

* "por Soleares" means "in the rhythm of Soleares."

LESSON 5—EXTENDED COMPÁS SEQUENCES

In the following examples, the chord progressions, techniques and musical structures introduced so far are combined and expanded into longer compás sequences. These are typical patterns used to accompany the flamenco dance.

COMPÁS POR ALEGRÍAS

The repeated slur from F# to E on the 1st string of the A Major chord is a very typical ornament in alegrías, and certainly underscores the joyous aire of the dance. Another traditional touch in this example is the tasty use of chromaticism (non-chord tones) on the E7 chord of the fourth compás (fourth system), and the sliding D and A chords of the fifth compás.

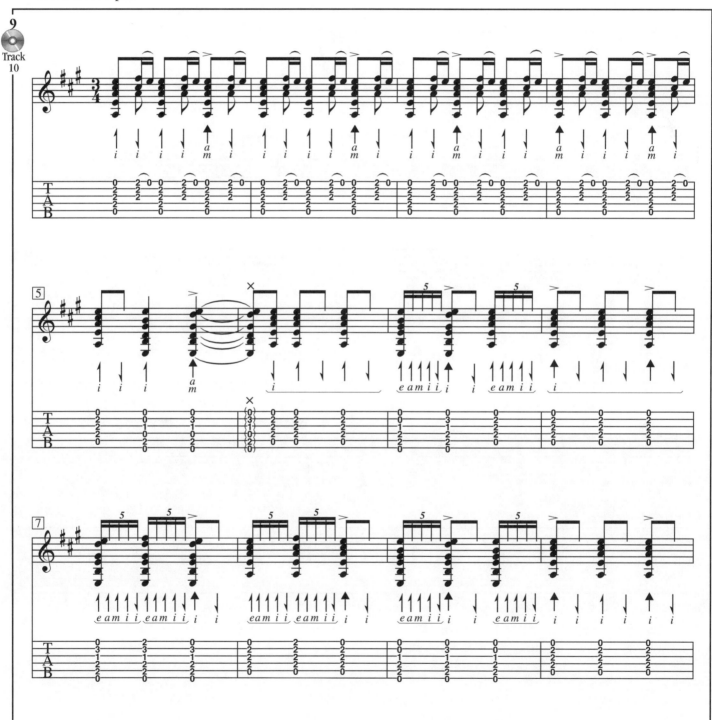

14

½CI = Half barre (three strings) at
the 1st fret
CII = Barre at the 2nd fret

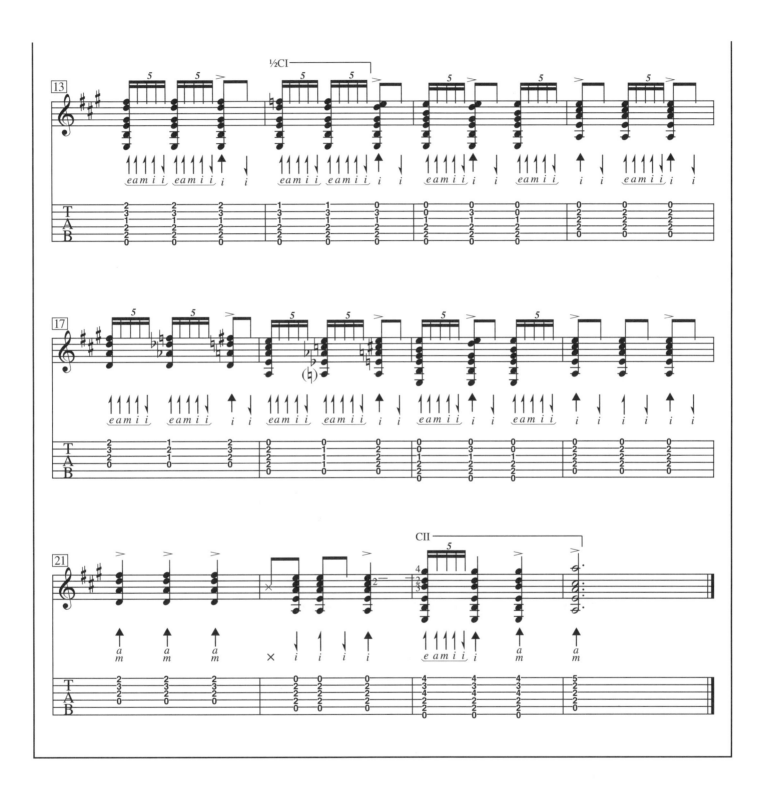

THE REMATE

As in example 9, the use of slurred ornaments adds authenticity and character to the compás sequence in example 10. You'll notice that three of the compáses in this example end with arpeggio figures instead of rasgueado on the 10th, 11th and 12th beats. This typical manner of ending a compás is called the *remate*, which literally means "re-kill," a rather gruesome term borrowed from bullfighting. Each flamenco form has its own distinctive remate that is its signature.

Note that both soleares and alegrías always end on the 10th beat of the final compás.

16

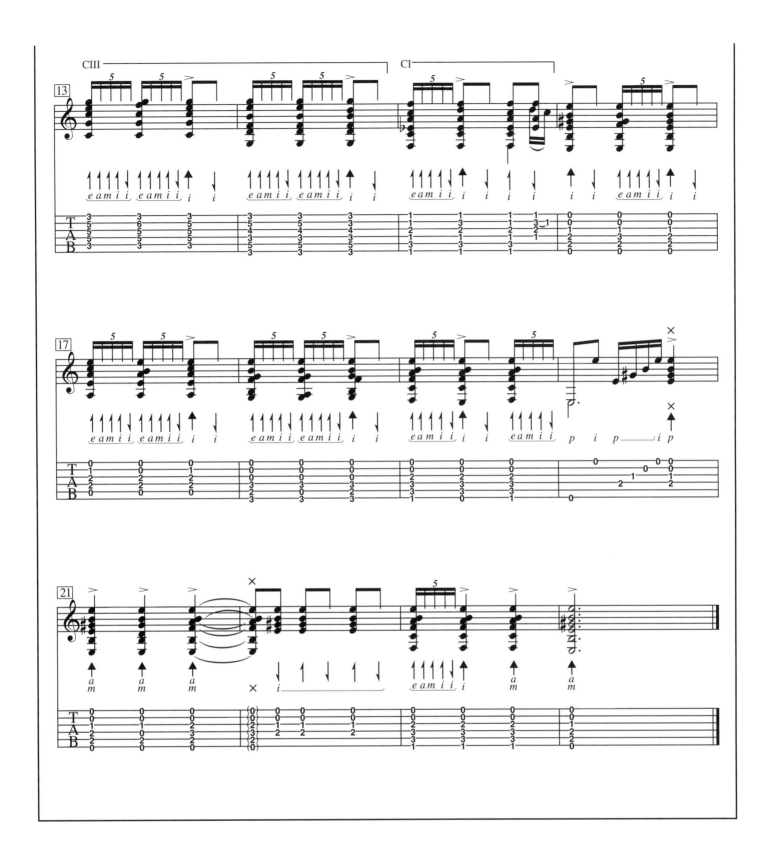

Bulerías is the most firey and exciting of flamenco dances. It is also the fastest version of the 12-beat compás derived from soleares. To reflect the faster tempo bulerías is written as a compás of 12 eighth notes rather than 12 quarter notes.

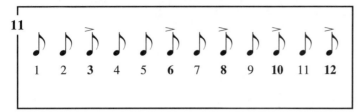

When seen in beamed eighth notes (example 12, below), readers with classical training will agree that the origin of this accent pattern (used for soleares, alegrías and bulerías) becomes more apparent.

HEMEOLA AND FLAMENCO COMPÁS

Examples of Spanish music dating back hundreds of years demonstrate alternating measures of two and then three accents. When expressed in eighth notes, both $\frac{3}{4}$ and $\frac{6}{8}$ will have six eighth notes per measure; the difference between the two meters is the placement of their accents:

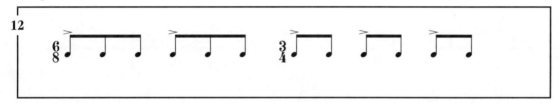

Alternating measures of $\frac{6}{8}$ and $\frac{3}{4}$ time is called a *hemeola* rhythm. Examples of this rhythm are heard in the opening bars of Rodrigo's *Concierto de Aranjuez*, in Gaspar Sanz's *Canarios*, and Leonard Bernstein's "America" from *West Side Story*.

The hemeola rhythm in soleares, alegrías and bulerías is not quite so obvious because the 12-beat phrase begins after the downbeat, and ends on a downbeat.

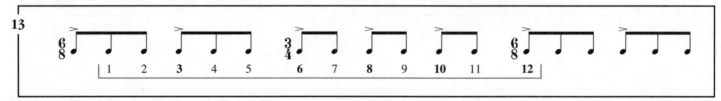

Unfortunately bulerías is very confusing to learn when written "correctly" in alternating bars of $\frac{6}{8}$ and $\frac{3}{4}$ time. To express bulerías rhythm as clearly as possible, we will portray each 12-beat compás as one bar of 12 eighth notes. We will not, however, use a $\frac{12}{8}$ time signature, since that does not accurately represent what is happening in the bulerías, either. There will be no time signature at all. Each eighth-note beat will be beamed individually, and the counting of each compás (with accents in bold) will be written below the TAB staff.

PLAYING BULERÍAS

In the Phrygian mode (such as from A to A with an F Major key signature—A–B♭–C–D–E–F–G–A), the most important chord change is ♭II–I: two major chords, one half step apart. The bulerías in example 16 is played in A Phrygian. The II chord is B♭ Major, played in a "flamenco version" that includes the open 1st string.

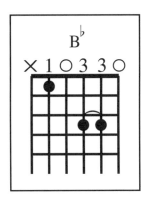

Since bulerías is played at a much faster tempo than either soleares or alegrías, the compás is expressed in much simpler beat divisions than are generally used in the slower dances. The compás of example 14, for example, simply uses golpes to mark the unaccented beats, and chords on beats 3, 6, 8, 10, and 12 are played with *i* upstrokes.

Bulerías can be easily learned if you conceive of the compás as two phrases of six beats.

14 **The First Compáse of Example 16**

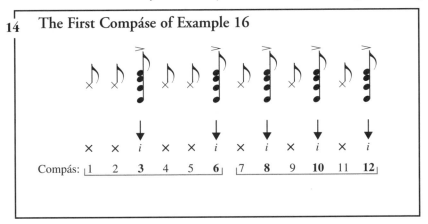

The compás below (example 15) is identical to the one above (example 14) except that the second half (beats 7–12) is elaborated upon with the use of two five-stroke rasgueados. Because of the quick tempo, one rasgueado is most often used to express two beats in bulerías. Be sure that the final upstroke of each rasgueado receives a full beat.

15 **The Second Compáse of Example 16**

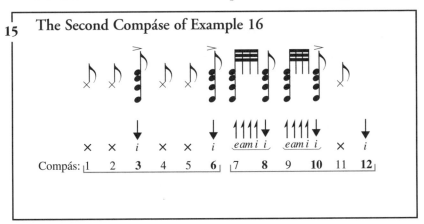

It is also important to note that a bulerías is often phrased from beat 12. Look ahead to the *Solo por Bulerías* on page 44. The fifth, sixth, and seventh compáses begin on beat 12, which is why the second and third systems have *open* measures at the end (no bar lines).

Example 16 demonstrates seven different ways to play bulerías compás. These variations are very much like a vocabulary. Master each of them individually, and then begin to interchange them freely. In this way, you will become fluent in the language of bulerías.

Bulerías, like soleares and alegrías, always ends on the 10th beat of the final compás.

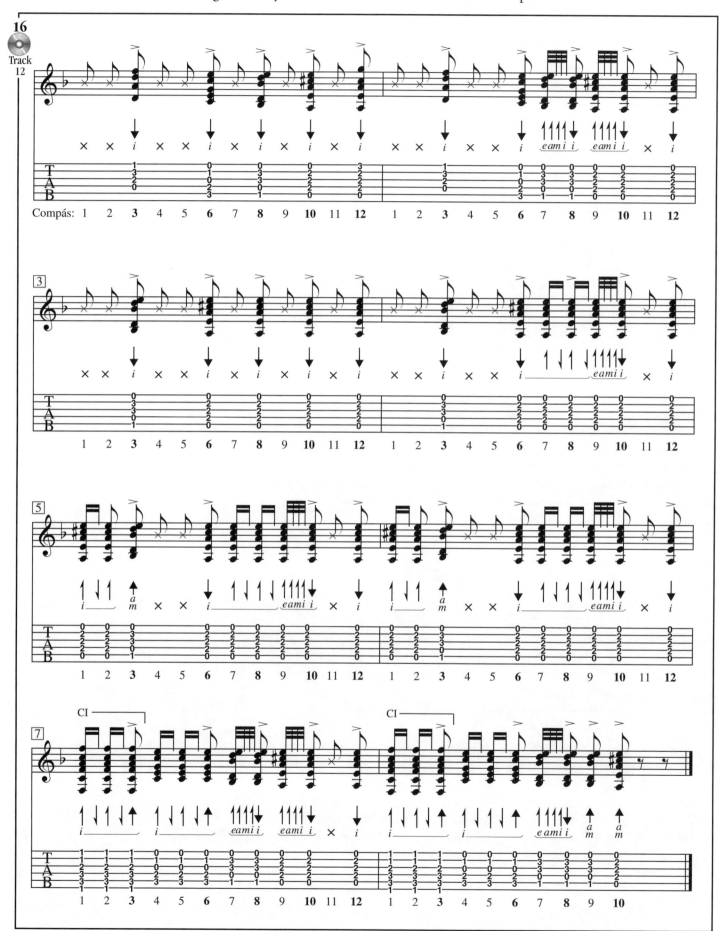

LESSON 7—OTHER FLAMENCO RHYTHMS

Soleares, alegrías, and bulerías represent one family of flamenco rhythms. Several others exist, and we'll sample some of these forms in this lesson.

LA FARRUCA

La Farruca, a folk dance from northern Spain, is in $\frac{4}{4}$ time and the key of A Minor. Although neither Gypsy nor Andalusian in origin, flamenco artists have embraced and performed La Farruca for more than a century.

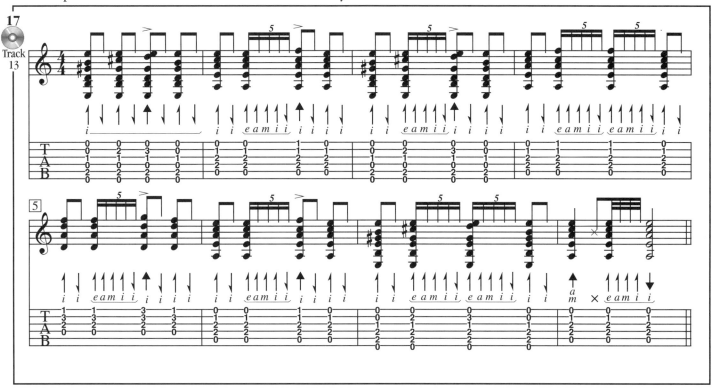

TANGOS

Tangos, by contrast, is pure Gypsy flamenco in $\frac{4}{4}$ time and the Phrygian mode. Even this short sampling of tangos demostrates a depth of expression La Farruca could never hope to approach. The eighth notes in this tango have a swing (uneven, long–short) feel.

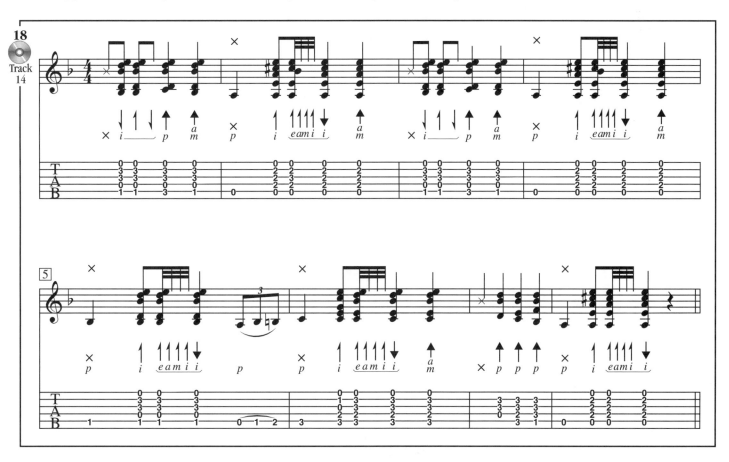

FANDANGOS

Fandangos are songs and dances that date back hundreds of years to the Moorish domination of Spain. Every region of Spain—nearly every city—has its own particular version of fandangos. Some forms of fandangos are strictly vocal and never danced (see lesson 12, page 32). When danced, fandangos are very much like flamenco waltzes—in $\frac{3}{4}$ time, and almost always with a golpe on the first beat of each $\frac{3}{4}$ bar.

Verdiales

A lively dance from Malaga, *verdiales* is one of the most familiar and frequently imitated Spanish rhythms.

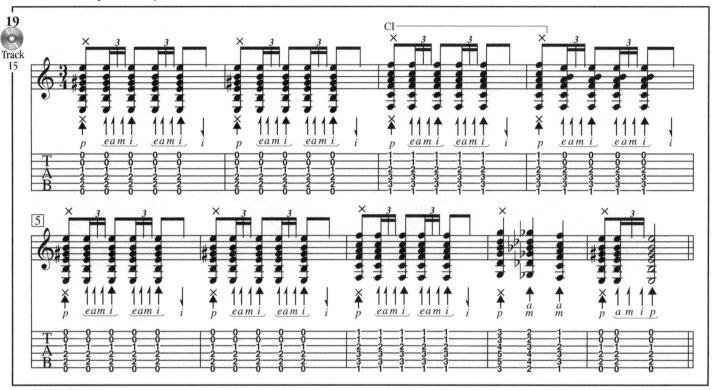

Fandangos de Huelva

Fandangos de Huelva is the most popular form of fandangos among flamenco artists. It is a more sophisticated and syncopated version of fandangos compás. Notice the use of indifinite ties to show that the chord continues to ring through the golpe.

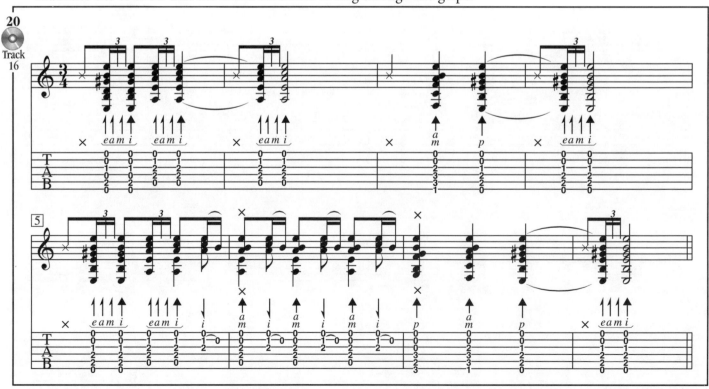

SIGUIRIYAS

One of flamenco's most profound and tragic expressions, the lyrics of *cante por siguiriyas* often question the very meaning of life. Siguiriyas has a very particular aire—a slow drag, which is never rushed and never used as virtuoso display.

The compás of siguiriyas is another variant of the hemeola rhythm. In siguiriyas, the compás begins on the second beat of the $\frac{3}{4}$ bar and is counted as five unequal beats.

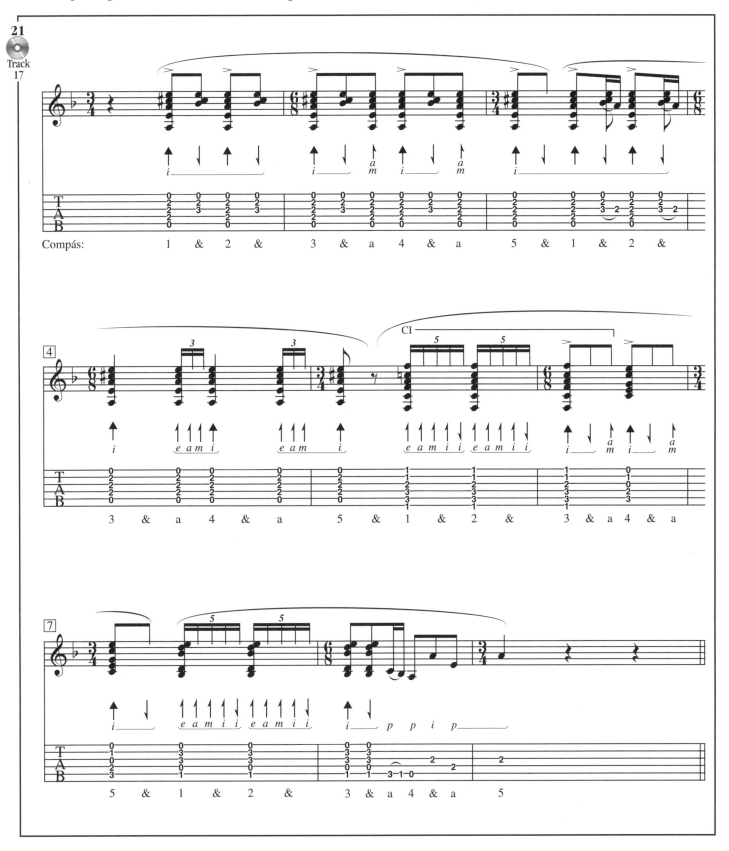

Chapter 2   FLAMENCO TECHNIQUE AND THE FALSETA

So far, we've only expressed flamenco compás through the use of rasgueado. In a sense, this mirrors flamenco history—the earliest role of the flamenco guitarist was to strum chords in dance accompaniment. But as the art of flamenco guitar developed, the musicians began to assert themselves by incorporating melodies into their chordal accompaniments. The melodies are called *falsetas*.

The earliest falsetas were undoubtedly simple melodies played with the thumb, but in the hands of the great flamenco guitarists of the 20th century, the art grew to encompass the full range of guitar technique. All manner of scales, arpeggios and tremolos were used to realize the full harmonic potential of the guitar fingerboard.

In this chapter, we'll explore the flamenco approach to these techniques and demonstrate how they are used to express both the rhythm and the emotional content of various flamenco forms.

LESSON 8—THE THUMB IN FLAMENCO

In the early history of flamenco, tiny small-voiced guitars were most often played in outdoor settings. To have their falsetas heard under these conditions, early flamenco guitarists developed the thumb technique of *apoyando* (rest stroke). While in most respects, the right-hand techniques of both classical and flamenco guitar are identical, a subtle but profound difference between the two is the use of apoyando thumb technique. Most classical guitarists rarely play rest strokes with the thumb, whereas in flamenco almost all thumb strokes are played apoyando. The flamenco hand position favors apoyando thumb work, a more arched wrist and more emphasis on hand and arm weight in the playing than is generally used in modern classical guitar technique.

The following examples explore various uses of apoyando thumb strokes, especially in combination with *i* free strokes. In these falsetas, allow the thumb to fall effortlessly yet weightily from string to string. Use gravity rather than force to play these falsetas.

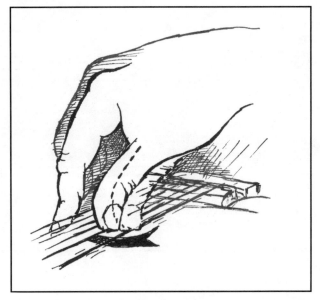

Rest stroke with p

POR SOLEARES

This falseta is very similar to the rasgueado compás in example 5, but expressed with *p–i* technique. The arpeggios on the first beat of each bar are played by gliding *p* from string to string until the high note of the chord, which is played free stroke with *i*. This technique produces a stronger arpeggio than is possible with *p–i–m–a* free strokes. The second compás of this example seems a repeat of the first until it is interrupted in beats 6 through 9 by a bass melody in ♩. ♩ rhythm. Bring out this melody with very strong apoyando thumb strokes.

Ramon Montoya *was one of the earliest flamenco virtuosos. He was born on November 2, 1880. Though born in Madrid, faraway from Andalucia, he developed the ability to play flamenco so well that by the time he was 14, he was employed in a Madrid cafe to accompany* cantaores *(singers). His virtuosity grew as fast as his fame. He began recording in about 1910. He was active as a performer until about 10 years before his death in 1949.*

POR ALEGRÍAS

Here, a simple bass melody in a triplet rhythm is played with thumb rest strokes. The open 1st string is a *pedal tone* (a sustained or continually repeated note) played with *i* free strokes. Interspersed within this pattern are flowing melodies played with as many slurs as possible. This is another very important aspect of flamenco guitar style that will be explored in many upcoming examples.

LESSON 9—ARPEGGIO FALSETAS

Ramón Montoya was most likely the first flamenco guitarist to play *p–i–m–a* arpeggios. His recordings document seemingly limitless arpeggio patterns on chord progressions covering the entire fingerboard. The importance of thumb apoyando carries over into arpeggio falsetas, the vast majority of which have arpeggio patterns accompanying apoyando bass melodies, as in example 24.

ESCOBILLAS POR ALEGRÍAS

Escobillas is a very important section of the dance alegrías in which the dancer displays spectacular heelwork. Escobillas means "brushes," describing a particular dance step. Example 24 is the most traditional accompaniment to escobillas. The melody is played entirely with apoyando thumb strokes.

POR SOLEARES

This example demonstrates two different versions of the most traditional of all soleares falsetas. In the first and second measures of both compáses, the 1st and 3rd fingers remain in place throughout the entire measure; the melody is played by the 2nd and 4th fingers. In the second compás, *ligato* (slurred) melodies are added to the traditional falseta. Be careful not to rush these slurs.

Some of flamenco's most virtuosic passages can leave an audience breathless but actually are not all that difficult to play. This is illustrated in beats 7, 8, and 9 of the second compás (found in the 3rd bar of example 25's second system). This spectacular lick combines a right-hand arpeggio with flowing left-hand slurs, one of flamenco's most popular and dazzling techniques. Place all fingers on beat 7, and hold them in position as long as possible throughout the measure.

POR BULERÍAS

Here is the slur/arpeggio technique applied to bulerías.

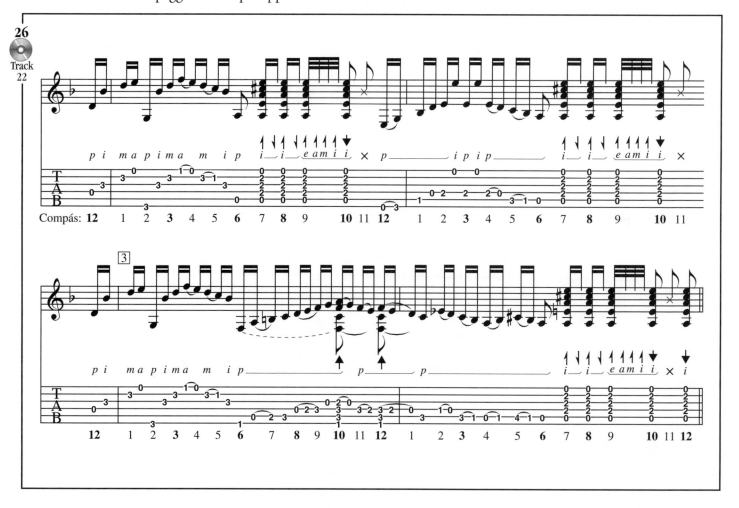

LESSON 10—ALZAPÚA

Alzapúa, a Gypsy word meaning "to raise the thumb," is another electrifying flamenco technique. Alzapúa combines a single-line bass melody with an accompaniment of downstrokes and upstrokes on chords, *all performed by the thumb*! The back of the thumbnail is used to execute the upstrokes.

Alzapúa is used in a variety of contexts and can articulate many complex rhythms, but the following three movements are the essence of alzapúa technique:

1) **Single note** — The melody note is always played apoyando. If the single note is played on the 6th string, the thumb comes to rest on the 5th.

2) **Downstroke** — The downstroke begins without the thumb lifting away from the 5th string. The downstroke is an arc-like movement in which thumb just misses the 1st string. The stroke is propelled more by forearm rotation than by thumb movement.

3) **Upstroke** — The back of the thumbnail hooks the strings in reverse of the same arc as the downstroke. Once again, forearm rotation turns the hand and thumb.

ALZAPÚA POR SOLEARES

This is the most traditional of all soleares alzapúa falsetas.

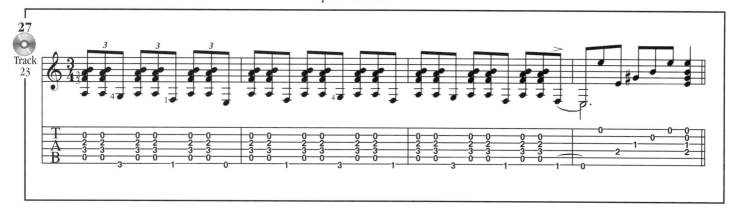

ALZAPÚA POR BULERÍAS

Here, the bass melody is elaborated with slurred figures between the down/up alzapúa strokes.

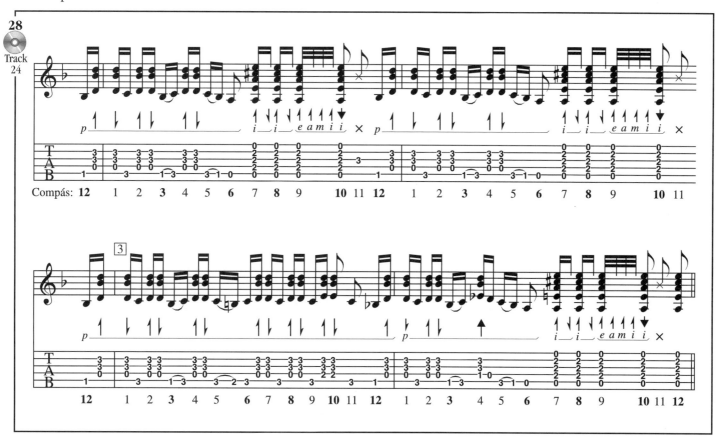

LESSON 11—FLAMENCO TREMOLO

Flamenco *tremolo* (in guitar music, this refers to rapidly repeated notes) completes the expressive range of flamenco guitar. Tremolo answers the rhythmic fire of rasgueado with the guitar's most singing melodic expression.

Using a technique borrowed from classical guitar, Ramón Montoya altered classical tremolo to create a new technique, which many listeners find even more beautiful then its classical counterpart. Classical guitar tremolo divides each beat into four equal parts: a bass note played with *p*, and three repeated melody notes played *a–m–i*. Flamenco tremolo adds an additional melody note, turning each beat into an even quintuplet fingered *p–i–a–m–i*.

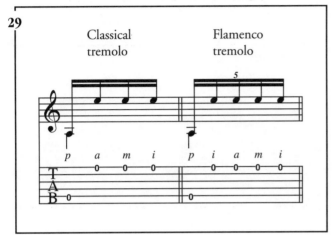

The flamenco tremolo has two distinct advantages over the classical: It can be played at a slower tempo without sounding mechanical; and its uneven beat division "fools the ear," creating its essential illusion of an unbroken melodic line.

One cannot rush mastery of tremolo. The secret to a great tremolo is not speed but *evenness*. If you are in a hurry to learn tremolo, practice very slowly. Focus your attention on dividing each beat into five exactly equal parts. Once a perfectly even quintuplet is achieved, tremolo can easily be brought up to the desired tempo.

POR ALEGRÍAS
This is a tremolo version of escobillas por alegrías.

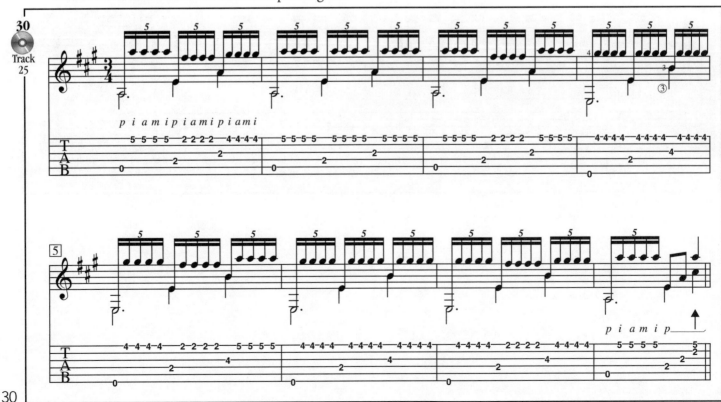

POR SOLEARES

This falsetta demonstrates how effectively tremolo can be used to express counterpoint between the bass and melody lines.

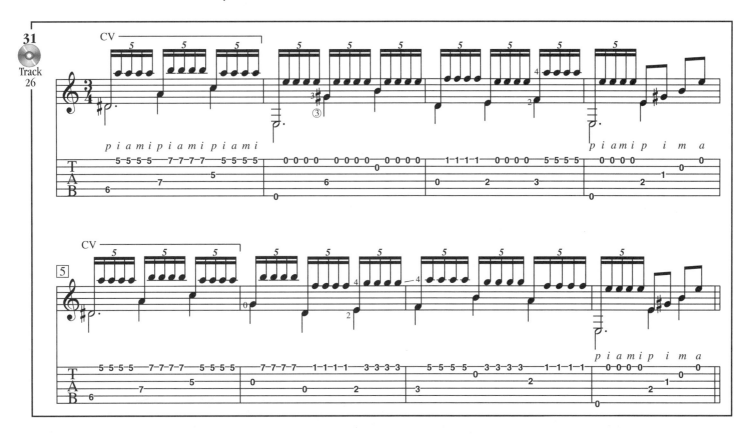

The author (far right) with Sabicas (center) and Mario Escudero (far left). If you look closely at the top of this photo, you may be able to detect where Escudero and Sabicas signed it. The photo was taken in New York City, in 1981.

Mario Escudero's *(b. 1928) compositional innovations ushered the art of flamenco into a new era. As a child, he studied classical guitar with Tarraga-disciple Daniel Fortea, and flamenco with the great Ramon Montoya. At age 14 he began touring the world as a guitarist for Spain's finest flamenco dance companies. Throughout the 1950s and '60s he enjoyed great international recognition as both a recording artist and a solo recitalist. The bold and sophisticated harmonies of his solo guitar works had a tremendous impact on Paco de Lucia, who called Mario Escudero "the Father of Modern Flamenco."*

Sabicas (Augustine Castellon) *(1912–1990) was unquestionably flamenco's greatest concert artist. His phrasing, tone, and effortless virtuosity were such that he could as easily be compared to history's great violinists and pianists as to other flamenco guitarists. A self-taught genius, Sabicas was famous throughout Spain by the time he was nine years old and was the first solo flamenco guitarist to tour the world. His concerts and the dozens of albums he recorded inspired guitarists from all over the world to learn flamenco, transforming it into an international art.*

In Lesson 7 on page 22, we mentioned that certain forms of fandangos are strictly vocal; they are never danced and have no rhythmic constraints. Singers improvise freely on each line of the verse in what is called *cante libre* (free song). When these forms are performed as guitar solos they are called *toque libre*. These are very free instrumental fantasies in which the entire expressive range of the guitar can be fully explored and exploited.

In this lesson, we will sample two extraordinary forms of the toque libre: *granadinas* and *tarantas*.

GRANADINAS

Granadinas are the fandangos from Granada. Its verses sing the praises of this beautiful and ancient city. A guitar solo for granadinas is often played in the key of B Phrygian (with a major tonic chord) and is characterized by long passages of flowing arpeggios and tremolos. The following example includes the traditional opening: tremolo figures written as grace notes (small, quick ornamental notes) played *i–a–m–i* that are followed by thumb strokes; arpeggios on the II and I chords (C and B); a typical cadence with the slur/arpeggio technique we explored in Lesson 9 (page 27); and the characteristic slide up the 6th string from F♯ to B, which is the "signature" of toque por granadinas.

Notice that the Libre section at the end is unmeasured; there is no specific time signature. You will hear this rhythmic freedom on the CD.

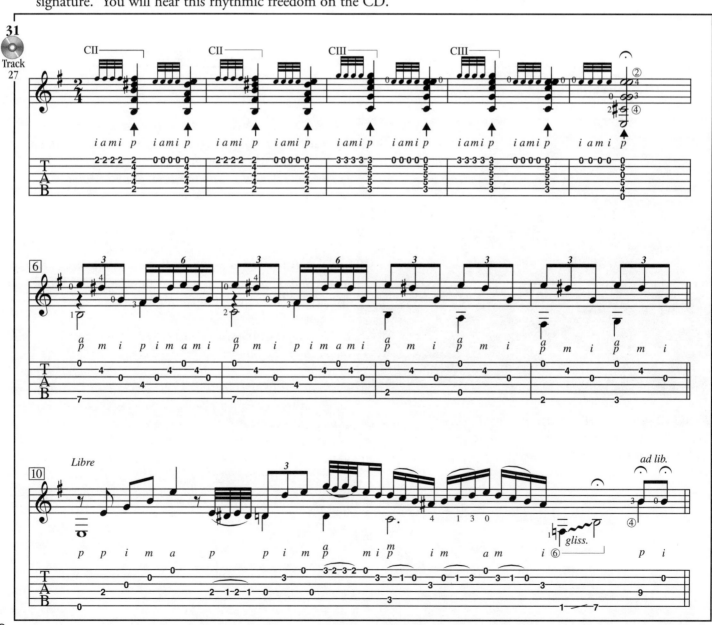

TARANTAS

Tarantas are among the darkest and most tragic flamenco expressions. The songs of the miners from the Linares region of Spain, the lyrics of tarantas describe the pain of young widows and the torture of a life deprived even of sunlight.

The anguish of the cante is reflected on the guitar with the use of the F♯ Phrygian mode. The open strings of the guitar clash with painful dissonance against the notes of the tonic F♯ Major chord. This short example demonstrates the extensive use of slurred passagework that is very characteristic of toque por tarantas. The desired effect here is not virtuoso display, but rather to have the guitar imitate the tortured wailing of the flamenco singer. These passages sound best when slurs are played as evenly as possible, allowing the notes of one string to overlap with the next. Because of the free nature of the taranta, no time signature is used.

Chapter 3   CONCERT SOLOS

SPAIN

FINAL WORDS

As a reward for your hard work learning the material in this book, we now complete our study with three full-length solos that incorporate all the rhythms, techniques and falseta styles you have learned. Before we begin to discuss the pieces themselves, let's consider their style and place in concert guitar literature.

In recent years, I've been delighted to see such prominent classical guitarists as Pepe Romero and Elliot Fisk include flamenco solos in their concert performances. To me, this trend makes perfect sense, since flamenco solos in the style of Ramón Montoya, Sabicas, and Mario Escudero, while rooted in folk culture, were conceived for concert performance. They are exactly analogous to the folk-inspired concert guitar music of Villa-Lobos, Ponce, Barrios, and Lauro, as well as the nationalistic (quite often flamenco inspired) piano works of Albeniz and Granados.

Since concert flamenco solos are exciting, passionate, highly virtuosic, and often very serious pieces, I must frankly admit that I'm surprised more classical guitarists—who are open-minded musicians always in search of significant new repertoire—don't fully embrace and perform concert flamenco. Throughout my experience as a concert artist I've found that flamenco solos are taken very seriously by music lovers and critics alike, and that audiences just love these dramatic guitar pieces.

An additional benefit of the style is that concert flamenco solos offer far more freedom than most classical pieces. The rules of compás must always be followed, but you have complete freedom to choose the falsetas and rasgueado styles that best suit your technique and temperament, and structure them into a solo of your own design. Most professional flamenco guitarists know dozens, even hundreds, of falsetas for every flamenco form. In concert, they will often draw upon this arsenal and spontaneously create new pieces composed of many carefully rehearsed falsetas they may have been playing for years.

The most important goal in performing a concert flamenco solo is to communicate the essential aire—the emotional character—of the song or dance on which it is based. Thus, your soleares should sound serious and reflective, your alegrías joyous, and your bulerías firey and exciting. In the following solos, you will find much that is familiar, but always slightly changed from the original falsetas or compás patterns you encountered earlier in this book. If some falsetas seem too difficult for your technical level, feel free to use the easier versions you learned earlier. Also, feel free to change the order of the falsetas, delete, or add material at will. Then share the thrill of flamenco guitar with your friends and with your audiences.

Solo por Soleares

picado = Flamenco scale technique.
Alternate *i* and *m*.

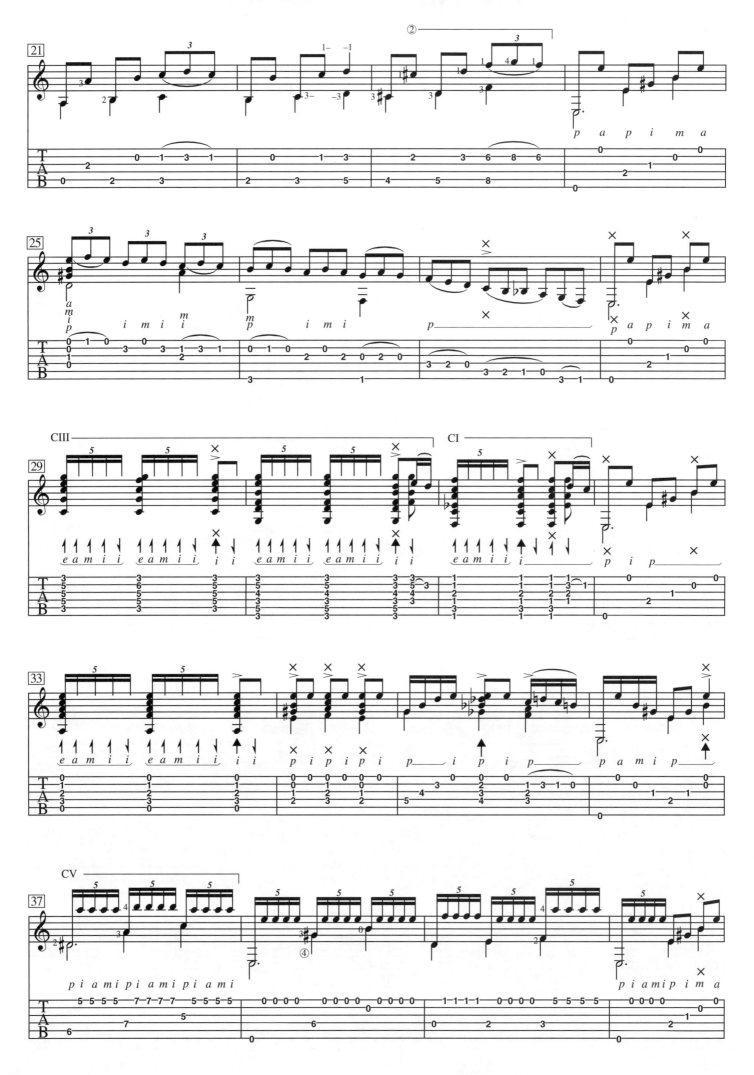

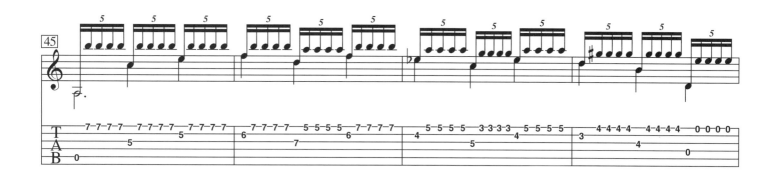

37

Solo por Alegrías

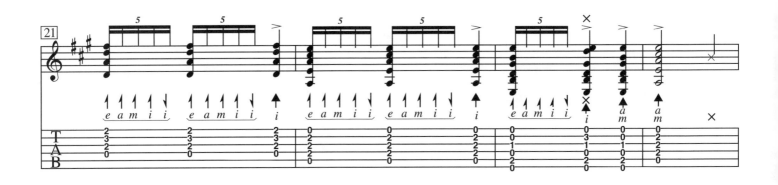

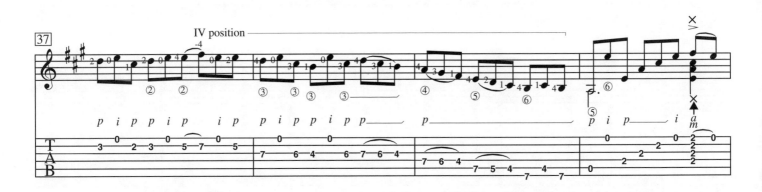

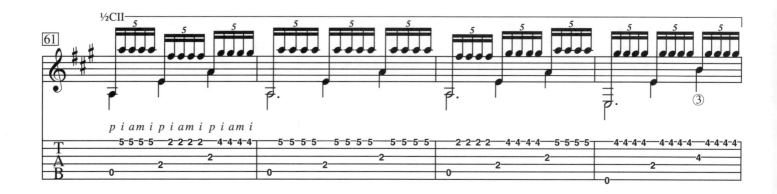

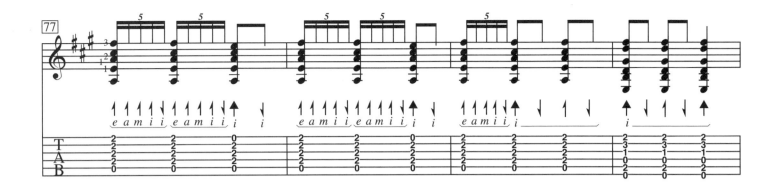

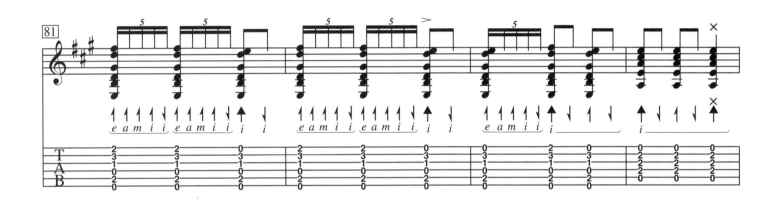

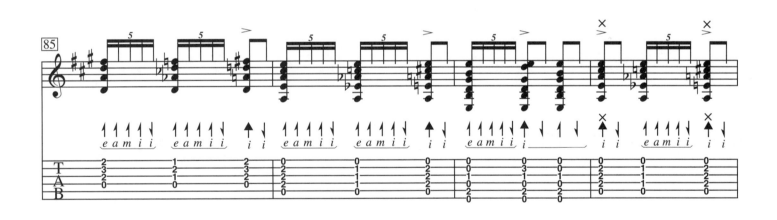

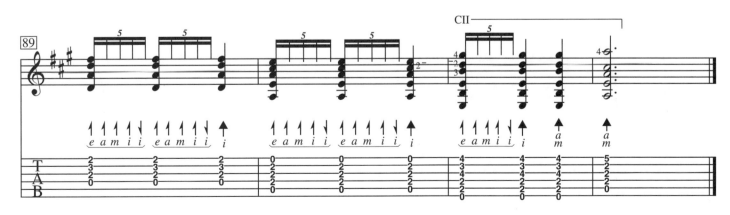

Solo por Bulerías

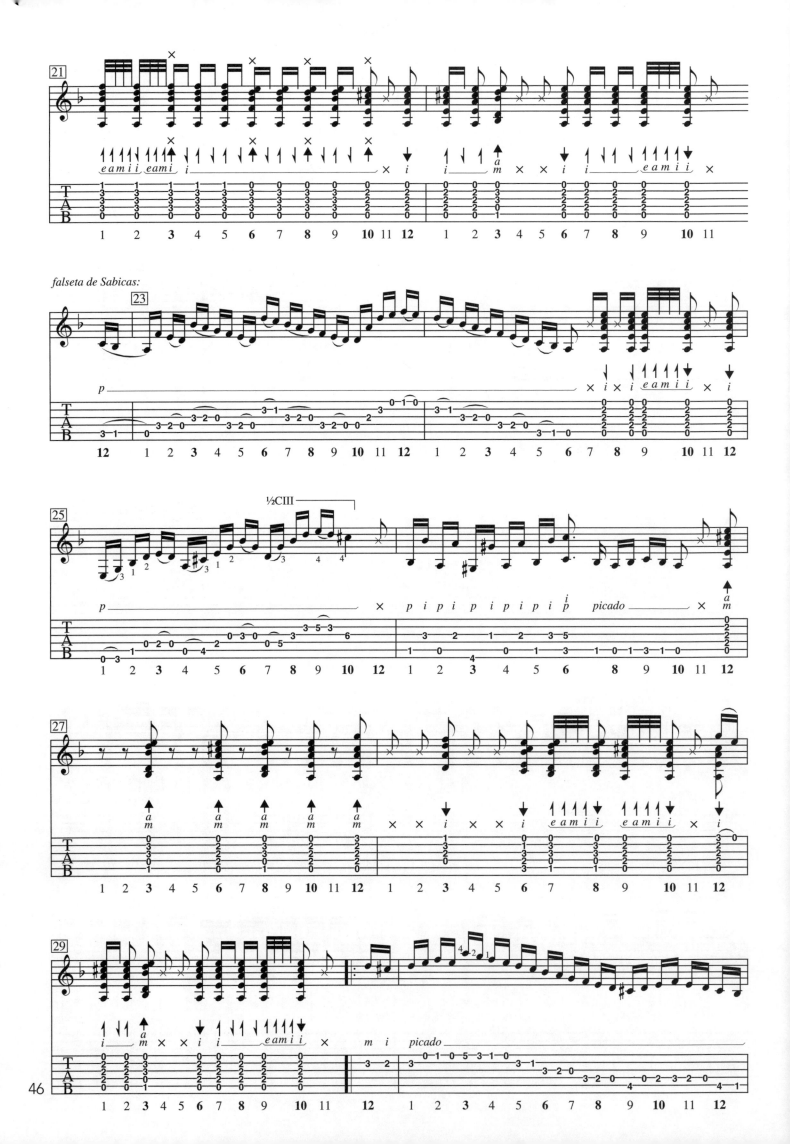

falseta de Sabicas:

46

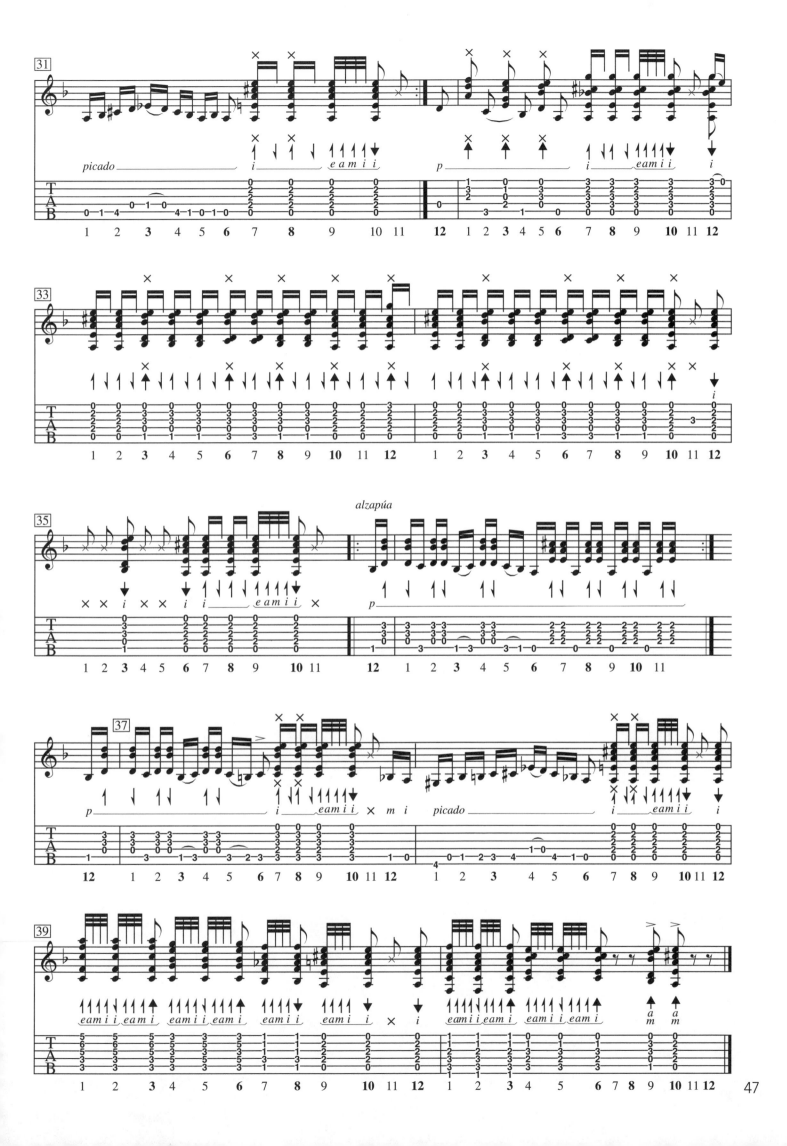